Contemporary Piano Literature

BOOKS 3-4

 Library for Piano Students

Selected and Correlated by Frances Clark
Edited by Louise Goss
Stories by Adele deLeeuw

Summy-Birchard Inc.
Miami, Florida

PREFACE

The *Contemporary Piano Literature* series is devoted to choice smaller keyboard works written by some of the composers who have achieved prominence in our time.

This series was designed as a companion to *Piano Literature of the 17th, 18th and 19th Centuries*. Together, the two sets form a representative collection of easier keyboard literature from the time of Bach to the present day.

Many of the pieces in the *Contemporary Piano Literature* books were written on commission for the *Frances Clark Library for Piano Students*. Others were taken from the repertoire of available contemporary works.

Frances Clark

Copyright © 1957 Summy-Birchard Music
division of Summy-Birchard Inc.
All rights reserved.   Printed in U.S.A.

SUMCO 6023
ISBN 0-87487-109-3

Summy-Birchard Inc.
exclusively distributed by
Warner Bros. Publications Inc.
15800 N.W. 48th Avenue
Miami, Florida 33014

TABLE OF CONTENTS

BÉLA BARTÓK
1881 - 1945

When Béla Bartók was only four he began to play with one finger on the piano many songs that he had heard and remembered. His mother gave him lessons and when his father died she supported herself by teaching. Young Béla made such progress that by the time he was ten he was helping to support his family by giving piano concerts.

He was one of the youngest men to enter the Budapest Academy of Music, and in spite of ill health he finished his studies with a brilliant record. Then he went to Germany and France to study further and to give concerts.

One summer, when he was vacationing at a friend's house in the country, he heard a servant singing songs that he had never heard before. This happened day after day, and he hid himself and wrote them down as they were sung. These, he discovered, were the real folk songs of the neighborhood, but they were so different from the other folk music he had heard that he wondered what else he might unearth in other parts of the country. He and a composer-friend, Zoltán Kodály, wandered from the Carpathian Mountains to the Black Sea, listening, putting down on paper, and finally publishing a tremendous number of authentic folk melodies.

In addition to many other types of music, Bartók wrote hundreds of short pieces for piano students. Many of them were based on these folk tunes he had found.

Bartók came to this country during World War II to stay for a short while, so he thought. But he stayed on and lived here for the last years of his life. In spite of illness and pain, he wrote some of his finest compositions. When Bartók's music was first performed in this country, it was hard for the audience to understand and appreciate it. But today his works are played and admired the world over.

The pieces which follow come from a set of student pieces called *First Term at the Piano* and from the first volume of *For Children*, a collection of Hungarian folk songs arranged for piano.

Children's Game

BÉLA BARTÓK

From "For Children," Vol. I

Play

BÉLA BARTÓK

From "For Children," Vol. I

Tempo I

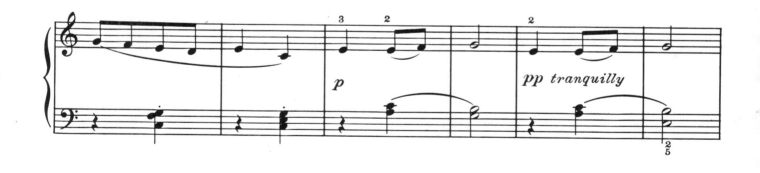

Teasing Song

BÉLA BARTÓK

From "For Children," Vol. II

Two Peasant Dances

BÉLA BARTÓK

Jeering Song

BÉLA BARTÓK

From "For Children," Vol. I

ALEXANDER TCHEREPNIN
1899 – 1977

At school in Russia Alexander Tcherepnin managed to slip manuscript paper between his books and during study periods found it much more interesting to put notes on paper than problems in arithmetic. He had learned to read notes before he learned to read the letters of the alphabet, and when other people gave presents at birthdays or special occasions he would write piano pieces— especially for members of the family—rather than go out and buy a gift.

His father, Nicolai Tcherepnin, was one of the best known conductors and composers of the nineteenth century. He gave his son his first lessons and it was soon evident that Alexander would be an outstanding musician. He liked to wait until his father left the house so that he could work out some of his own ideas at the piano.

He studied later at the St. Petersburg Conservatory in his native city under some of the finest musicians in Europe. Before long he began giving concert tours in many European countries, in Palestine and Egypt. These were so successful that he made two tours around the world, including visits to China and Japan.

While he was in China, Tcherepnin became very interested in the native folk music and stayed long enough to study it. It was here that he met and married Lii Shiaunmin, one of China's leading women pianists, and together they have given frequent concerts of Chinese music.

During his travels Tcherepnin came to the United States sixteen times to play, conduct and lecture. On one of these visits he was invited to teach piano and composition at DePaul University in Chicago.

Tcherepnin has written almost every possible kind of music—songs, operas, ballets, orchestral music, band music and a great deal for the piano. His compositions are filled with humor, energy, lyric melodies and lively rhythms. The pieces in our collection were commissioned in 1954 for the *Frances Clark Library for Piano Students.*

Prelude

ALEXANDER TCHEREPNIN

Moderately, tranquil

The Clock

ALEXANDER TCHEREPNIN

Hide and Seek

ALEXANDER TCHEREPNIN

With spirit

Valse

ALEXANDER TCHEREPNIN

Merry-Go-Round

ALEXANDER TCHEREPNIN

Old Tale

ALEXANDER TCHEREPNIN

DMITRI KABALEVSKY
1904 -

One of Russia's leading composers, Dmitri Kabalevsky, was born in St. Petersburg when Tcherepnin was five years old, and two years before the birth of Shostakovich.

Kabalevsky's father was a civil servant. It was not until the boy was fourteen and the family had moved to Moscow, that he had any real music lessons. Then he was enrolled in the Scriabin School to study piano. After that he went to the Moscow Conservatory to study composition with the famous Miaskovsky, and at the same time he began teaching at the Scriabin School.

He started composing seriously when he was twenty-one, and in five years had written a string quartet, a piano concerto, and many songs and piano solos. Much of this was done during lulls in battle while he was at the front in the second World War, and one of his best known works, *People's Avengers*, for chorus and orchestra, was written in collaboration with a young poet who was also at the front.

Today he lives in Moscow and teaches composition at the Moscow Conservatory. His works have won two of Russia's highest prizes, the Order of Merit and the Stalin Prize.

Kabalevsky has written operas and ballets, music for the movies, stage and radio, and works for orchestra, chorus, chamber groups and piano. An important part of his work is his piano music for children. For several years he taught in a government school for children. He was distressed over the lack of suitable teaching material in Russia at that time and set about to compose pieces which would be easy to read and to play, and yet would help children learn to love fine music.

The pieces in our collection are samples of the music he wrote for his own students.

A Cozy Waltz

DMITRI KABALEVSKY

From "24 Little Pieces," Op. 39

A Little Song

DMITRI KABALEVSKY

From "Children's Pieces," Op. 27

Simply singing

The Clown

DMITRI KABALEVSKY

From "24 Little Pieces," Op. 39

Fast, with humor

Toccatina

DMITRI KABALEVSKY

With motion

From "Children's Pieces," Op. 27

Sonatina

DMITRI KABALEVSKY

From "Children's Pieces," Op. 27

With motion

Dance on the Lawn

DMITRI KABALEVSKY

From "Children's Pieces," Op. 27

DOUGLAS MOORE
1893 - 1969

Douglas Moore's first production was a dramatic play which he presented in the attic theatre of his parents' home on Long Island. Overturned chairs covered with rugs represented mountains, and the script included a romantic proposal and three murders. He was seven years old! With the box-office receipts of five cents he bought an American flag to use in other productions.

He took piano lessons at an early age, and he says that one of his greatest ambitions was to play a Liszt rhapsody. But a still greater pleasure was to compose music of his own—which he did during his practice hours!

Oddly enough, it wasn't until he was a young man of seventeen that he heard his first Beethoven symphony, and the experience was a thrilling one. At Yale he had no opportunity to pursue his study of music until his junior year, but then he studied intensively and returned to Yale after graduation to study composition.

He wondered, after his service in the United States Navy, whether he should devote himself entirely to music. Did he have enough talent? As a trial he set to music three poems by his friend, Archibald MacLeish, and asked him to decide. MacLeish recognized the quality of Douglas Moore's work and said Yes. From then on Moore devoted himself to furthering his career in music—study in this country, in Paris, and an appointment to the staff of the Cleveland Museum of Art as curator of musical arts and as organist.

His early love of acting lured him to take part in the plays at the Cleveland Playhouse, and for a while it seemed as if he might become an actor instead of a musician. But when he received the Pulitzer Prize which made it possible for him to go back to Paris, music became his sole aim. He developed a distinctive style when he became aware of his own country's vigorous early days. One of his most delightful compositions is *The Pageant of P. T. Barnum,* based on the life and times of the circus showman.

The two pieces which follow were commissioned in 1956 for the *Frances Clark Library for Piano Students.*

Decoration Day

DOUGLAS MOORE

The Princess and the Pea

DOUGLAS MOORE

A drowsy waltz

Faster and agitated

D.S. al Fine

Escalator

DOUGLAS MOORE

DMITRI SHOSTAKOVICH
1906-1975

It was wartime. Dmitri Shostakovich's Seventh Symphony was being performed in the Hall of Columns in Moscow. Suddenly the wailing of sirens pierced the stillness. Enemy aircraft was trying to penetrate to the capital. The concert continued. At the last mighty chord the audience sprang to its feet, shouting and applauding. A man appeared on the stage to warn the people that an air alert had been sounded. But no one left the hall. The people were completely under the spell of this music that had been written for and about them. Shostakovich, lanky and bespectacled, a lock of hair falling over his high forehead, was pulled to the stage, where he had to take bow after bow.

He had not always been so popular. While he was a student at the Leningrad Conservatory, he had written many fine works and by the time he was nineteen had composed his first symphony. It was performed a year later before a distinguished group of critics and a fine career was predicted for him. But after five more symphonies and some operas, he composed *Lady Macbeth of Mzensk*, which was condemned as 'vulgar' and 'a menace to true art.' Even his ballet, *The Limpid Stream*, was attacked as 'frivolous and over-simplified.'

So Shostakovich began to change his style, and to write music for the people, music based on war and heroism, and the ideal of freedom, as he saw it personified in his country. His popularity returned, and during the war his music became almost a battle song of Russia and her western allies. He became known throughout the world, and in Russia he is looked upon as a national hero.

He lived in Russia and taught at the Conservatory where he studied as a boy. He is known for his interest in young students and his encouragement of their talent. He has written operas, orchestral music, chamber music and piano music, as well as music for theatre, ballet, dance bands and the movies. Among his piano works is a little album called *Six Children's Pieces,* from which the following selections are taken.

A Sad Fairy Tale

DMITRI SHOSTAKOVICH

From "Six Children's Pieces"

The Mechanical Doll

DMITRI SHOSTAKOVICH

From "Six Children's Pieces"

CYRIL SCOTT
1879 - 1970

Poetry and music has been woven together all through Cyril Scott's life, and many countries have influenced him.

His father was a Greek scholar, and his mother was a gifted amateur musician. The young English boy played the piano by ear at an early age and his mother encouraged him. When he was seven he began to compose. His parents sent him to Germany to study piano at the Hoch Conservatory, but because he was so young—only twelve—he had a tutor come to his house each day to help him with his studies, instead of going to a regular school.

He returned home for a while, keeping up with piano studies, and then went back to Germany to concentrate on composing. While he was there he made a lifelong friendship with a young German poet, Stefan George, who opened up to him the world of poetry; and later, when he had gone back to England and was giving piano recitals and lessons to piano students, he began to write poetry himself. His first verses were published the same year that his first composition was performed in public.

Cyril Scott liked to use multi-rhythms in his music, which means frequent shiftings from one rhythm to another. He made many interesting experiments in harmony, too. Although he was trained largely in Germany, there are influences of France and the Orient in his work. One of his most delightful compositions is a musical setting of *Riki Tiki Tavi*, the hero of Kipling's *Jungle Book*.

Scott wrote a great many small works, as well as several operas, church music, and compositions for chorus, voice and piano. *Seesaw* and *March of the Tin Soldiers* come from a set of ten student pieces which Scott originally called *Young Hearts*, but which has been renamed *For My Young Friends*.

Seesaw

CYRIL SCOTT

From "For My Young Friends"

March of the Tin Soldiers

CYRIL SCOTT

From "For My Young Friends"

Reprinted with the permission of the publisher.
From the collection *For My Young Friends*.
Copyright 1920 by Elkin & Co. Ltd.

ALEXANDER GRETCHANINOV
1864 - 1956

Alexander Gretchaninov's father was a humble shopkeeper in Russia, and he wanted his son to become a business man, too. But his mother had more artistic understanding, and it was through her efforts that young Alexander discovered the world of music. She insisted that the father buy a piano so that their children could take lessons. Alexander was entranced with the instrument, picked out melodies with one finger, then with five, then with both hands. He was determined to become a musician, and his mother encouraged him even against his father's wishes. Afterwards, a family friend persuaded the father to change his mind.

The school he attended had occasional evening concerts, and there he listened to a string quartet for the first time. He did poorly at grammar and other subjects, but at seventeen he drove a bargain—if he were allowed to enter the Moscow Conservatory, he would promise to supplement his musical studies there by teaching himself in other subjects.

The famous Arensky at the Conservatory told him bluntly that he had not much talent and would do better in something else. Gretchaninov solved that by entering the rival conservatory at St. Petersburg! There he came under the influence of the great composer Rimsky-Korsakov, who gave him help and inspiration. One of Gretchaninov's best-known symphonies is dedicated to Rimsky-Korsakov.

After leaving the Conservatory he began to support himself by giving piano lessons. In spite of this he had time to do a great deal of composing—much of it for church choruses. No one, it is said, knew better how to use the human voice for artistic expression. He had a rich gift of melody, too, and his songs are famous for their Russian style and their lyric tenderness.

Gretchaninov has written symphonies, chamber music, operas, vocal, choral and piano music. Like Bartók, he was interested in folk music and based many of his compositions on folk songs and dances. The pieces in our collection are taken from an album of piano pieces called *Glass Beads.*

Morning Walk

ALEXANDER GRETCHANINOV

From "Glass Beads," Op. 123

Little Beggar

ALEXANDER GRETCHANINOV

From "Glass Beads," Op. 123

My First Ball

ALEXANDER GRETCHANINOV

From "Glass Beads," Op. 123

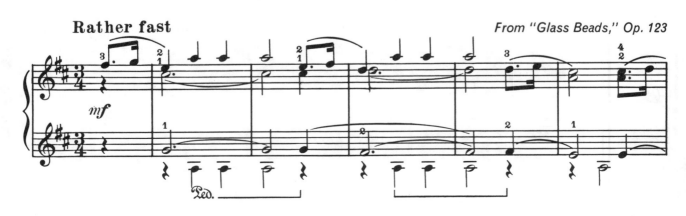

On the Bicycle

ALEXANDER GRETCHANINOV

From "Glass Beads," Op. 123

Waltz

ALEXANDER GRETCHANINOV

From "Glass Beads," Op. 123

Moderately

ROSS LEE FINNEY
1906 -

Ross Lee Finney's mother used to rock him in rhythm to poetry she read or to folk songs she sang. When he was six he would sit at the piano with the Bible upside down on the music rack, and improvise little pieces, pretending to read them. His mother, a pianist, gradually taught him what musical notation was, and helped him write down the notes he was playing.

His brother Theodore played the violin, his older brother Nathaniel the trumpet, and he started on the cello at ten. They were living then in Valley City, North Dakota, and he has vivid memories of the family playing the music of Schumann and Schubert together, with the fire glowing on the hearth and the blizzardy winds howling outside. Music, he says, has always meant family to him far more than concert.

When the family moved to Minneapolis his musical life centered in the University. He, his brother and another student organized a piano trio and gave concerts all over Minnesota. He had to wear an old-fashioned dress suit, which he hated. But on one occasion when he took a bow and his trousers split, he was more than grateful for the coat's long tails!

Later he taught cello at Carleton College, and there he met his future wife. There have been years of study in Europe and at Harvard, years of becoming established as a professional musician, and years of teaching at various large colleges in the East. Now he is professor of composition and composer-in-residence at the University of Michigan.

His works for string quartet, orchestra and piano have been widely performed in this country and in Europe. The pieces which follow are the first things he has written for young pianists. They are reprinted from an album called *25 Inventions*, published in 1957.

There and Back

ROSS LEE FINNEY

Lively

From "25 Inventions"

Berceuse

ROSS LEE FINNEY

From "25 Inventions"

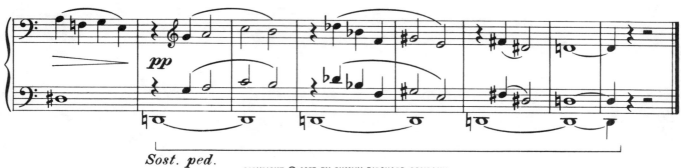

Skipping

ROSS LEE FINNEY

From "25 Inventions"

Reflections

ROSS LEE FINNEY

From "25 Inventions"

IGOR STRAVINSKY
1882 - 1971

"I compose," said Igor Stravinsky, one of the most important leaders in twentieth century music, "because I am made for that and cannot do otherwise." He believed in inspiration, but did not wait for it. For him, composition was a daily function which he had to discharge.

The man whose music caused near-riots when it was first performed, who has been praised and misunderstood and argued over, was slight and thin, with nervous gestures and penetrating eyes behind strong lenses. He had great energy and led a vigorous life.

As a boy he grew up in a musical atmosphere. His father was the leading bass in the Russian Imperial Opera; his mother was a trained pianist. He often went to the Opera to hear his father sing, and early on learned to read and enjoy the scores. In the winters there was the exciting musical world of St. Petersburg; in the summers the family went to the country where young Igor heard stirring national folk songs which were later to influence his music.

His father wanted him to study law because it was a safer career than art. But when Stravinsky met Rimsky-Korsakov and studied under him, he was encouraged to give up law for music. For the wedding of Rimsky's daughter, Stravinsky wrote *Fireworks* and sent it as a surprise to the master. It was a great blow to have the package returned unopened because of Rimsky's sudden death.

A lifelong friendship with Diaghilev, the impressario of Russian ballet, brought both men fame. For Diaghilev, Stravinsky wrote numerous ballets, which established his reputation and influenced the development of modern music.

Stravinsky wrote many piano compositions; but very little for student pianists. The selections which follow come from an album called *The Five Fingers*.

Lento

IGOR STRAVINSKY

From "The Five Fingers"

58

Moderato

IGOR STRAVINSKY

From "The Five Fingers"

Larghetto

IGOR STRAVINSKY

From "The Five Fingers"

With rocking motion

SERGE PROKOFIEV
1891 - 1953

"I bumped my head against an iron trunk when I was three years old," Serge Prokofiev tells us in his autobiography, "and the bump stayed for something like twenty-five years. A painter who did my portrait said, 'Perhaps your whole talent is in this bump!'"

Wherever it was, it manifested itself early. He improvised a little piece when he was five. It was in F major—but minus the B-flat, because he had a fear of touching a black key! A year later he was able to write down his new compositions, and at nine had completed an opera, *The Giant*—all in piano score, without orchestration—which was produced for the family on his uncle's estate.

At twelve the precocious Prokofiev had an audition with Glazunov who was highly impressed with the boy's talent and suggested that he enroll in the St. Petersburg Conservatory. For his examination he produced a portfolio of four operas, two sonatas, a symphony and a number of piano pieces. Nicolai Tcherepnin, the father of Alexander, was one of his teachers, as was the great Rimsky-Korsakov.

While he was a young man, Prokofiev was best known as a pianist. He won the Rubinstein award and the Piano Prize, traveled widely, gave concerts, and conducted his own works in Russia and abroad.

"You are a revolutionary in music just as we are revolutionary in life," the Minister of Education said to him, "and we ought to work together. But if you want to go, we will not stand in your way." After touring Siberia, Japan, and Honolulu, Prokofiev eventually came to the United States, where he was regarded as very much of a musical curiosity because of his modern thinking. He stayed five years, and while he was here had a commission from the Chicago Opera Company to write an opera—*The Love for Three Oranges*.

The pieces in our collection come from an album called *Music for Children*, which he wrote especially for piano students.

March

SERGE PROKOFIEV

From "Music For Children," Op. 65

Rain and the Rainbow

SERGE PROKOFIEV

From "Music For Children," Op. 65

Unhurried